Silicon
Alley

Milton Benson, Jr.

Copyright © 2021 Milton Benson, Jr. ALL RIGHTS RESERVED

This book or any portion thereof may not be reproduced or used without the expressed, written permission of the publisher except for the use of brief quotations in book reviews.

Written by Milton Benson, Jr.

Editing & Layout by J. Cerrone Smith

Book Design & Cover by Milton Benson, Jr.

ISBN 979-8-9851239-0-6

Atlanta, GA

Table of Contents

Introduction

Peace and many blessings, family. First, I want to thank you for embarking on this journey with me. This project, which started about three years ago, was inspired from a consultation I had with my mentor and friend, holistic practitioner, Malikah Ali. I told her I love to write short stories and poems, but I hadn't written anything in a few years. Of course, she asked why. My response was because I was unable to focus. These weren't her exact words, but she basically told me that if it was something I love to do, then I should try and find some time to do it. Also, that doing the things you enjoy is good for your mind and body.

So, I made the time to write the first poem and I shared it with her during our next meeting. She really enjoyed the poem and said it was revolutionary. When she said that, I thought about great writers and revolutionary icons like Marcus Garvey, James Baldwin, Dr. Langston Hughes, Dr. Maya Angelou, Malik El Hajj

Shabazz, Dr. Huey P. Newton, Fred Hampton, and Bob Marley. I immediately felt the responsibility to dig deep, to give my contribution to the fight for justice and equality for my people.

I chose the title of the book *Silicon Alley* because, Silicon Valley is home to some of the biggest technology companies in the world. As we take a broader look into reality, technology has taken over our society. We the people are the subjects in their billion-dollar scheme. So, as Black people faced with so many odds in this tech driven society, we are like in an alley fight with everyone else. That would be those whose objective is to destroy everything or anyone of us who succeeds.

So, without further ado, I present this collection of poems to you.

Milton "*June*" Benson, Jr.

America's Ghetto

There is a kid somewhere in the hoods of Brooklyn, the Bronx,
Chicago, Detroit, Oakland and Harlem;
who looks out his bedroom window every day, and says, "I'm
gonna make it out of here.
I'm gonna make something of myself because I can be anything!"
Then those sirens from afar, that are all so familiar growing up in
the hood, ring out.
Maybe somebody got shot today.
Or maybe a car accident, or a domestic violence dispute, or maybe
a robbery that took place, or a drug bust gone down,
Or there is a fire somewhere.
Life in Ghettos of America;
the survival of the strong,
a place where the weak perish slowly,
or quickly,
depending on the season.
The summer sun is beautiful but deadly;
cool nights can be loud and ruthless,
parks can be filled with children playing,
or gang members bonding,
or syringes by the sliding board.
Does America even know we exist, or she doesn't even care?

As far as I know, she blames us for our conditions.
The world views Lady Liberty as a fairly fit woman.
Well, I view her as obese,
fattening her belly with the work from slaves.
Power and greed are her delicious addictions,
and this overindulgence has made her sick.
This condition has created an environment: the ghettos of America.
She is the sole owner of her sickness, and the results show that
somewhere in the hoods of Brooklyn, the Bronx, Chicago, Detroit,
Oakland and Harlem, there is a kid who looks out his bedroom
window every day, and says, "I'm gonna make it out of here.
I'm gonna make something of myself because I can be anything!
And against all odds, I am gonna win!"

A Quiet Place for a Man to Cry

Imagine, just imagine, for a brief moment,
A six-foot hole dug in the earth,
never covered, still open.
Or three-inch nails being hammered in your back,
or a policeman's gun placed on your temple.
Or in a blink of an eye, caught in a shoot-out,
or your view from inside of a cage.
Or having to stand naked, emasculated, for a visit to see loved ones.
Or an entire world of people, but you feel entirely alone.
Or to find out as a child you are not special,
or as a child beg for God's help.
Or your dreams are now nightmares,
or some days you feel like a King and some days you feel completely worthless.
Or criticized for not being perfect,
or the subject for annihilation.
Or the pressure of being a father,
or the pressure of a son.
Or Superman with no super powers,
or placing a planet on your back.

Or a bullseye for arrows aimed at your heart,
or the mirror you see when you look at slavery.
Or the expectations that must be met, HAVE to be met,
or all the people you have disappointed.
Or the struggle just to breathe in a world of smoke,
or to find someone who can relate,
or to find someone who will be in love with you,
or to find someone to actually love.
Or to let the wall you've built come down,
or to be betrayed by an angel.
Or to silence the anger hidden deep inside,
or to smile in the face of pain.
Or to find some peace when there is none,
or to find some place to cry when there is no crying allowed.
OR TO FINALLY REALIZE, YOU'VE BEEN SILENTLY
CRYING, YOUR WHOLE ENTIRE LIFE!

Beautiful Evil

A pose so breathtaking you can't look away,
with a kiss from the wind it dances ever so sweet.
The radiant sun gives life and helps resurrect its essence…
it's pristine Elegance.
When you look at trees you see a creation of beauty, a pawn.
A part of the ecological system.
Sometimes I see a tool, a tool that was used for a noose.
Bloody leaves dripping,
bodies hanging,
Who would think laughter, excitement, adrenaline, and cheering,
would describe pure hate, pure evil?
Listen to the screams, crying, pain, helplessness.
The crack of a whip…
The flesh tearing…
The rain beating…
The sun baking…
The eyes bulging…
The castrations conducted…
The tongues seized…
The buck breaking…
Humanity violated…
Violations justified…

Scriptures converted into weapons…

Poison on papyrus…

Racist rhetoric…

Lies concealed…

Vision tainted…

Identity erased…

Freedom with chains…

Words spoken…

Codes decrypted.

The birth of a being made to feel subhuman,

made to feel inferior.

Psychologically destroyed…

DAMAGE CONTROL COMPLETE.

Now let's call them African Americans.

Awake

I am here, breathing, seeing, hearing, tasting and feeling.
I am present,
a part of the Universe,
a part of the Earth.
I can hear her heartbeat,
I can enjoy some of the wonderful things she has to offer.
I am present,
I witness the beautiful, sunny days that remind me of adolescents running around in the park.
I can reach out and touch the drops that land on my hand when it rains.
I can look at the gray skies of Buffalo and
trek through the many inches of snow.
I can see the clear night skies in Atlanta with its stars sitting and watching the earth.
I am present,
I can hear the colony of birds, posted on a tree in front of my sister's apartment window every morning when I stayed with her in the Bronx.
I can fight through the crowds on the packed MTA Green line trains to and from work.
I can taste the delicious African food we had when we ventured out

to D.C.
Or the cheesesteak subs in Philly,
I am present.
I can hear the sadness in her voice when she looks back,
or the laughter while watching our favorite shows.
I can smell the homeless living on the streets of New York,
or chicken from the fast food joints smothering the whole block.
Take a deep breath, inhale,
then slowly exhale.
Close your eyes and then gradually open them.
I am present!

Ascension

Let the spirit awaken,

Let the body evolve,

Let the Conscious face the music,

Let reality be the horror show,

Let self speak to self,

Let the lies be punished,

Let the disease die,

Let the blood boil,

Let the skin toughen,

Let the evil be killed,

Let the sorrow be released,

Let the lens come into focus,

Let life exist but be not present,

Let silence be your sword,

Let the door slowly shut,

Let the rain flood the earth,

Let the present mind free,

Let the soul once again be planted,

Let the roots dig deep,

Let the foundation be unshakable,

Let the sun shower energy,

Let the spirit reawaken,

Let the love cascade in,

Let the peace cover you like a woven blanket,

Let the strength march forth,

Let the invitation of Supreme Being embrace you,

Let self fall in love with self,

Let the knowledge walk through the Gate,

Let the happiness be not disrupted,

Let society feel your presence,

Let the God in you be born.

Footsteps of God

The Universe is me.
Black derived from carbon,
melanin sparkling beauty,
360 a message, a path, a journey.
A star glimmering in the heavens,
a word spoken to man.
Pure is the heart, pure is the soul,
free within spirit.
But a wandering eye will eventually see the beast,
an evil whisperer enticing,
chains pulling you closer and closer to the edge.
A cry for desperate help, for strength, for survival,
for aids to come for this immaculate event.
Do you believe? I repeat, do you believe that within you there is a light?
A light that radiates farther than the galaxies.
An extension of ominous encapsulates you.
Look beyond the flesh, look beyond the horror this world has given you.
Be still, be silent,
be the archer holding the high ground.
Prepare for the internal war, prepare for the exterior battle.

Now walk lightly into the fray.

But before you engage,

about face and witness the footsteps of God.

My Allegiance

On this day I pledge allegiance,
to my melanated Blackness.
And I always want you to remember,
Black Power from January to December.
We keep searching for the Holy Ghost,
while insanity is sitting at the command post.
When are we gonna realize we are a reflection of God,
and the white Savior is nothing but fraud?
That's why my flag is red, Black and green.
I don't need a ghostwriter,
I'm the architect of this sixteen.
Oh, beautiful America…
You got scars upon your face,
for the crimes you've committed against an entire race.
We continue to fight for equality in a free land,
We continue to die on battlefields for a country that for us won't take a stand.
We continue to be imprisoned while others walk away from their rightful punishments.
Where is the Justice? Where are the indictments?
So, we must hold the mirror accountable…

Invest in ourselves so we can become more knowledgeable.
Unroll the Dutch and make reading an addiction,
stop letting social media be your distraction.
Blackness coming from a different angle,
in my mind's playlist I deleted the Star Spangle.
Don't fight the fact these diamonds is coming from God.
My message, my gift, my life may be hard…
But I am the reflection of He…
So, I be…
The designer of my reality.

Dear God

I hit you up a few days ago,
I'm still wondering, had you blocked me a few years ago?
Seems like I never get any clear answers.
Maybe I'm not asking the right questions…
I'm living in a sick world of sin,
I'm trying to build myself from within.
I'm not a hero but I'm trying to save the youth,
Willing my inner soul to see some growth.
God, please forgive me for my past mistakes,
I can't stop them, but I hate going to wakes.
I know it's a reminder of the inevitable, and that life is beautiful
and incredible.
I still remember as a child crying,
"why am I alone?" I kept asking.
Wondering what sin I committed to lead me to this life of struggle
which eventually transported me to the barbed jungle.
I dearly begged for your aid,
Day after day on my knees I prayed,
No one came, no one came…
The white picket fence I dreamed was a fantasy…
The pissy staircase in the projects was my reality.
Hand-me-down clothes, holey sneakers, and braces…

I was beat down in lack of confidence…

Contemplated suicide…

Scared of life. Scared of death.

I chose otherwise.

As this journey continues and life keeps recycling,

I will continue to strive… continue to love…

Continue to keep walking, continue to keep calling.

I don't know how much grain is still left in the hourglass,

so, I'ma stand on Black Power till the boarding pass.

Sometimes this life feels too much to bear,

But I believe in you, God,

and I'm truly sincere.

Mind Psychology

The Black American family…
We know what pain is,
we know what struggle is,
and we know what hurt is.
We don't crumble or deteriorate,
we cope and adjust to our circumstances,
which is like a growing poison in the subconsciousness.
Which Americans know more about trauma than us?
Are we really Americans, when everyone else, if given the chance,
would vote "nay?"
How do you repair a broken mind?
How do you search for self if you don't even know self?
The world has painted us as a monster,
no allies, no real home to call our own.
The hate runs so deep, we turn on ourselves…
We think bleach is a solution.
Straightening the hair, weaves, blond hair, and different color eye
contacts.
We flee from our origin.
We have been programmed to despise each other.
Your Blackness is ugly or your Blackness makes you think you're
better than my Blackness.

Silence this suicidal madness!

Where are our stories?

The narrative before the kidnapping,

rapes and torture?

One of the worst crimes we committed was to not relay the story of our tribe.

The umbilical cord severed,

a history written for us.

Attacking our self-pride,

the core of our soul.

A broken man begets a broken woman, and in turn births a broken family.

Skyscraper

Born and raised in the heart of Mecca,
the projects was my skyscraper.
Who says the sun don't shine in the hood?
Yeah, there's shootouts, drugs; and if I could've left I would.
But the roots grew from a boy to a king,
Papa worked forty plus, now I'm doing the same thing.
I look over my shoulder and see a scared teen,
scared to live, scared to die, scared to dream.
Sometimes I wonder, "how did I get to this place?"
It's sad some Black folks love to put on Black face.
Cancer got my family in heartaches,
while the system giving my people headaches.
Black Power running through my veins,
toxic mentality in the hood causing pain.
It took experience to finally realize,
that truth will triumph over all lies.
Man trying to duplicate pyramids in the sky,
can't believe the Black God did it, so he deny,
and try to build towers, claiming he got supreme powers,
but falling short to his evil desires.
I got good and bad memories in the PJ's,

Concentration Camps Designed to keep the aboriginals' progress delayed.
I built a fort around my pain for a decade,
when the lion left the cage he had to face the blockades.
Today in Harlem the forecast is sunny and blue,
Momma I'm still walking through the projects coming home to visit you.

Slaves in the Land of the Free

We've been called animals,
We've been called "super predators,"
We've been called stupid,
We've been called lazy,
And we've been called Niggas.
Did we adopt this face?
Crimes against humanity forced us to this place.
We went from tribes to a race.
Did we feed an opinion?
Can an oppressor really understand oppression?
Can a devil really love an angel?
Was I included in the Star Spangle?
Why do we keep looking for the world to see slavery from a different angle?
From a lens seeking love for humanity...
Not bloodshed, white insanity...
Or a demon posing as a missionary?
CAN YOU DEFINE HATE?
A word , an emotion with attachments that can lead to violence, resistance or silence.
You hated me for over four-hundred years, then you ask why I

don't trust you now...
But the real question is: how can you still hate me even now?
I was just driving my car with my family and I had a registered gun...
I mean all I wanted to do was go to the store to get some skittles...
I was on the block minding my own business not selling anything...
I was driving from Illinois to Texas to start a new job...
I was playing with my toy in the park...
Just being a kid, just being a kid...
Your crimes have shown how far you would go to take me off the grid.
And since my life is no longer a bid, you'd just rather get rid,
Of my existence, my creations and my beautiful history, feeding my people lies and mystery.
You controlled the people by concealing their true origin, their true wealth.
But the blind has fought to know thyself,
as we awake, as we rise like the Sun...
We are one with the universe,
not a plague nor a curse...
But an evolving force,
slowly elevating ourselves to be in tune with source...
Taking control of our course.

So, yes…

We've been called animals,

We've been called "super predators,"

We've been called stupid,

We've been called lazy,

And we've been called niggas.

But we've also been called Kings, Queens and Gods.

UNDERGROUND
RAILROAD
N
BUFFALO
NEW YORK

Soul of Africa

Our ancestors relayed messages through songs, through dance, through music.
This is our code, our language, our soul...
The rhythmic step that enters the body...
Energy that flows...
Sound waves that dance...
Heart that steady beats...
The thump that pounds like the stomping of a tribe.
The pulse and our soul are one.
We effortlessly intertwine the step.
It is embedded in us...
It is a part of us.
It speaks to our beings.
It sings to our spirit.
Can you hear a joyful clap in unison?
A foot that stomps, that taps?
Notes that glide on a scale?
A body gracefully painting a work of art?
Muscles contracting...
Breathe, stretch, reach...
I can still hear that Jambe...

I can still hear my Ancestors…

I can still hear Africa.

The Judge

God please help me with this verse,
let the evil in my heart disperse.
Give me the Almighty strength to fight,
and when that day comes lead me to the light.
With this free will man has enslaved me.
With this free will my choices made me.
I'm struggling in a land of riches.
The scars of slavery are too deep for stitches.
Black is a color and society's crime.
You can't understand Black experience through a book or a rhyme.
Let history finally unfold,
and let all the lies be exposed.
Black Power is a nightmare for America,
"Black Power" – words echoed from Our ancestors.
Laws were created to judge me, walls were built to confine me, stories created to deceive me.
The world was seduced to turn against me, including my own brother and sister.
The gatekeepers lust to relive the power of their ancestors.
The court is fixed,
the jury be my savior or my worse critics.
What do you see when you see me?
Or do you even see me?

Does my life matter?

Did her life matter?

I see your pretty wings Sandra…

Fly my Queen…. Fly.

The Design

The Black Woman,
The rib,
The design,
The scent,
The beauty,
Our Companion,
We are connected forever.
For we crave her presence,
Her touch, her voice, her spiritual warmth.
Her octave that is like a hummingbird singing gracefully into our ears.
The unwavering support she may give, but often undetected.
The look she gives can stop time, draw you in and penetrate your soul...
Speed up your heart rate, make you yearn for more.
The Black Woman,
The rib,
The design,
The scent,
The beauty,
Our Companion,
We are connected forever.

She's a compassionate teacher steering our life's journey...
Nurturing you, young and old.
Comforting with a warm hug, kiss or a beautiful sparkling smile...
Incubating, bonding, surviving the womb.
The detachment to attachment.
I lay upon her breast...
We completed a term to start another...
My first love,
A love unbreakable,
My guardian angel till death...
Been a part of me from the beginning...
By accident or by will.
The Black Woman,
The Rib,
The design,
The scent,
The beauty,
Our companion,
We are connected forever.
You complete me as you should!
As you were commissioned to do so,
by the Greatest Architect in existence.
Please forgive me for my shortcomings,

As I may not measure up to your checklist,

But check this…

We were made for each other…

We embody each other.

I can only fully understand you as you can only fully understand me.

We bleed together, we fight together and we march together.

We survived a horrific journey together.

The tides didn't break us,

the shackles didn't break us,

the overseer's didn't break us,

Jim Crow didn't break us.

Evil and hate will never break us, for we stand tall, strong and full of love…

Together.

So, I salute you my Queen…

Mother Earth…

Let's Continue our Journey,

Together…
The Black Woman,
The Rib,
The design,
The scent,
The beauty,
Our companion,
We are connected forever.

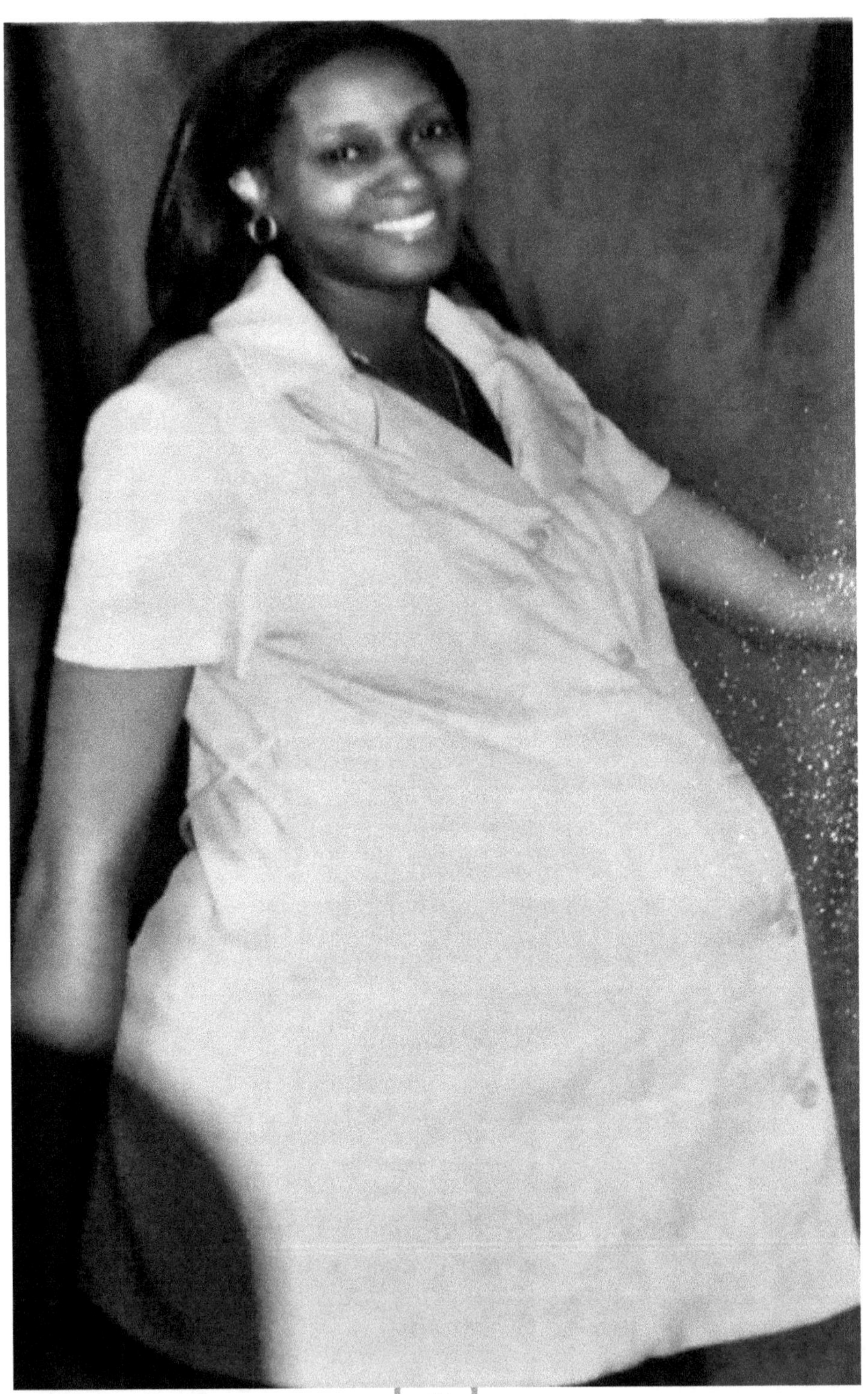

The Watcher

I was chosen.
I was introduced, to a light at about two years of age,
married to his soul I was.
A child is born innocent and angelic.
He held tight, attached to his mother's hip,
holding on for dear life.
Fearing and absolutely terrified of the world, I shadowed his every waking day.
His mother and him were inseparable.
This connection and way of life was enjoyable, and safe for him,
shielded from the world,
until one day, there were mentions of school and other kids.
That very first day was dreadful for him.
She kissed him upon his cheek,
tried to convince him it will be alright.
Gave him a hug as he was crying, terrified.
She stayed with him a few minutes and then left.
The beginning of a life-long journey.
From my observation this necessary pushing out of the nest, may have caused withdrawal.
Over the years he developed emptiness, loneliness, anger and

insecurity.

I observed him as a pre-teen and as a teen walking to and from school, sometimes just barely holding on.

Sometimes asking for God's help, his protection, his love, sometimes questioning where was all that he had asked for.

Why was he not present in his life?

Sometimes wanting to end his existence.

He took long walks alone to Randall's Island,

Wishing to walk away into another life...

A life where there was happiness, love amongst all people, smiles, and an abundance of life's pleasures.

No ghettos, no homelessness, no drugs, no thieves, no hate, no shootings, no murders – no evil!

The inner tomb of a child can be an immaculate mansion, or a wretched dungeon.

I watched and watched as hopes and dreams slipped away.

I feared for him many a day,

wanting to intervene, to lift him up,

give him hope, maybe give him another day.

But the slope was too steep...

He lost his way.

Then eventually was captured, enslaved, shackled and caged, by a system that forages on Black men.

Once again he prayed...

Prayed for survival, prayed for help, prayed for strength.

I don't know what's to become of him under these circumstances...

But I hope his prayers will be answered.

I will keep watching, because I am only a watcher...

A watcher is who I am.

Who Am I?

I am a Black Man,
Born in Harlem,
Born a King,
Born a problem.
Born in a society filled with hate,
One life struggle,
One life great.
Is African my identity when Africans don't even like me?
Black scars from the plantation,
My allegiance, to the Black nation,
My ancestors kidnapped,
Treated like animals made to live a life trapped.
Look at my nose, look at my lips, look at my face…
A sculpture of pure elegance.
You can't get rid of me because I refuse to die.
Who am I? WHO AM I?
I am a young Black rebel,
A son of God here to fight evil.
I am a master of self, healer of health, builder of wealth.
I am a compassionate teacher,
Poetic artist, a preacher,

A spiritual being, elevating,
Flying, and experiencing life as it unfolds...
Whether walking down that narrow or straight road,
Who am I?
I am me, I am energy, I am love
I am part of the Universe...
I am conscious, I am struggle, I am strong, I am peace...
I am time, I am who I was meant to be...
I am on a journey,
I am life, I am beautiful,
I AM BLACK!

Who Has Love for the Black Man?

The Black Man is one truly unique specimen.
Created by the Almighty,
definitely a blessing.
This vessel linked to the motherland,
my bloodline's homeland.
Can you imagine, if there was no God?
In the afterlife being mistreated, discriminated against, and barred from Paradise.
The color of my skin comes with a price.
Fighting to exist twice.
The color of my skin is not the hue of my character,
As melanin is correlated to dark matter.
I strive to be my self-master,
I stand here beautiful, Black,
With a Black Queen with a machete who got my back.
Numbers replace names for felons…
When they come home from serving time they try to get their life back…
Struggle to find employment, struggle to adjust and live…
Struggle to be in a position to just give…

Wanting to contribute to his Queen and kids,
Or like heroic soldiers decorated with medals,
Purple stars on the battlefield
But back home still considered niggers.
Where's my liberty, oh, Lady Liberty?
Oh, I soon remember you were defaced.
Even as a gift your Blackness was a disgrace.
Your beauty wasn't American enough.
Your contributions will never be good enough.
I still see blood stains on my pillow.
I still see blood stains on my coat.
Who was the last slave off the last boat?
I keep a lookout waiting for my mule and my land...
Who has love for the Black man?

Trapped

I feel trapped in an evil world.
Disgusting moralist zombies feeding off the weak,
the pious and the humble.
Justice is more like just us.
Where do we hide?
Where do we stand?
Where do we direct our voices that usually descend on deaf ears?
Maybe we should sign...
Use that form of communication to breach the heartless.
We're insecure, trying to survive the day...
Never trusting...
Never able to walk into our full potential of love for humanity.
God, the earth is sick,
A deadly disease has plagued it,
We see it, hear it and feel it...
What can we do?
Man has used your words against us.
That trickery you speak of,
Warning the pious of an evil that lurks,
That whispers,
That smiles,

That laughs,
That greets you in the dawn of the morning,
And seeks to lynch you at night.
My brother killed my brother,
My sister envies my sister,
My Blackness may not be Black enough,
My Blackness is not white enough.
I feel the venom for the human race invading my thoughts and my heart.
I battle with inner peace,
Fighting to be released from this cage,
Trapped.

Transition

I woke up this gray morning…
A Saturday…
Usually a day of adventure in the city, but today wasn't the usual.
It is a day, that I have been all too familiar with.
A shave and a soothing shower as I begin,
I put on my best then set out on my quest.
Multiple trains, transfers, glaring out the window, occasionally watching people with a somber mood.
I eventually arrive at my destination…
Greet countless members of family,
sharing hugs, handshakes and warmth from family I haven't seen in years.
As I approach Grand Pa,
he is dressed in a suit.
He looks at peace, resting from the strenuous path.
He is now engulfing on a new one,
a spiritual direction.
Ninety years he borrowed a physical vessel…
It will return back to its essence.
The family share their experiences with him,
some funny and some valuable life lessons.

I listen to the eulogy, finally realizing I will never see him in the physical again.

My heart saddens.

I can still hear his voice in my mind,

and I Wonder is he alright?

Has he been reunited with Grandma, Auntie Helen and Uncle Lawrence.

I was given a gift to have him for over four decades of my life.

He was there as a source of strength when I was clinging on to my sanity in a cage…

Sitting across from me telling me stories of his father.

I am so grateful for our bond.

We eventually get to the cemetery where he will be joined with Grandma.

We say our last goodbyes and watch as he is lowered into his final resting place…

His term complete.

His spirit and memories will live on.

Farewell King!

Zion's Militia

This is a life...
A life repeated...
Through generations...
Psychological deconstruction opposed on the human mind:
less than, ugly, lazy, worthless, dumb, dirty, sexually obsessed.
The conscious is fed a script, an idea, an opinion that has been visually and verbally hammered into the brain over and over and over and over through media, movies and music...
Platforms used as weapons of mass destruction...
Until the sub conscious believes this is me, this is who I am.
But there is a Light.
Where there is evil, there will be good,
This is the balance of the Universe,
So, march forth, Zion's Army!
The legion of rebels who have broken the chains of mental enslavement.
Fought self in an epic battle...
Scratched, clawed and was reborn.
Now enlightened, armed with knowledge of self, pride and beautiful vessels.
Ready to engage...

Ready to teach…

Ready to change the course of history…

Stand up against injustice…

And reclaim the Kingdom.

Knowledge, resilience and strength be thy weapon,

Proceed to march forth, Zion's Army!

In Loving Memory of

Milton Sylvester Benson, Sr.

(1944-2019)

www.ingramcontent.com/pod-product-compliance
Ingram Content Group UK Ltd.
Pitfield, Milton Keynes, MK11 3LW, UK
UKHW021925190726
13853UKWH00002B/857